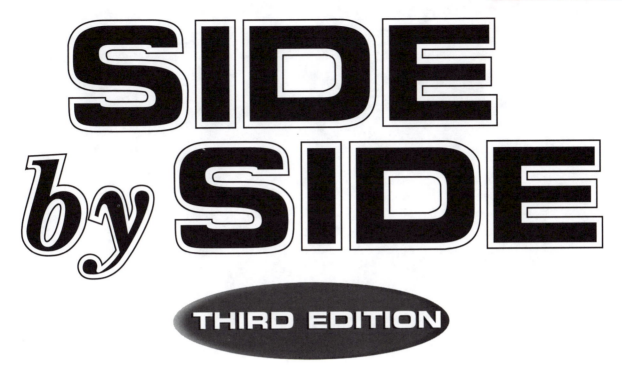

# SIDE by SIDE

**THIRD EDITION**

# Testing Program 3

Steven J. Molinsky
Bill Bliss

*Contributing Author*

Robert Doherty

Longman

longman.com

**Side by Side Testing Program 3, 3rd edition**

Pearson Education, 10 Bank Street, White Plains, NY 10606

Vice president, director of publishing: *Allen Ascher*
Editorial manager: *Pam Fishman*
Vice president, director of design and production: *Rhea Banker*
Associate director of electronic production: *Aliza Greenblatt*
Production manager: *Ray Keating*
Director of manufacturing: *Patrice Fraccio*
Associate digital layout manager: *Paula D. Williams*
Interior design: *Paula D. Williams*
Cover design: *Monika Popowitz*

Illustrator: *Richard E. Hill*

The authors gratefully acknowledge the contribution
of Tina Carver in the development of the original
*Side by Side* program.

ISBN 0-13-026885-2

3 4 5 6 7 8 9 10 -TCS- 10 09 08 07

| Student's Name _____ | I.D. Number _____ |
| Course _____ | Teacher _____ | Date _____ |

## CHOOSE

*Example:*

What are my sister and her friend _____?

a. study
b. studying
c. be studying
d. studies

**1.** What _____?

a. do he read
b. is he read
c. is he reading
d. does he reads

**2.** _____ to the movies?

a. You like to go
b. Do like you to go
c. Do go you to
d. Do you like to go

**3.** Dorothy is busy. _____ a sweater.

a. She knits
b. She's knitting
c. She knitting
d. She's knits

**4.** _____ scrabble very often?

a. Are you playing
b. Do you play
c. Are you play
d. Are you be playing

**5.** What kind of music _____?

a. is she composing
b. she's composing
c. she composes
d. does she composes

**6.** _____ whenever he can.

a. He's exercises
b. He's exercise
c. He exercises
d. Does he exercise

**7.** _____ the players on our team practicing now?

a. Our
b. Are
c. When
d. Do

**8.** _____ Mr. and Mrs. Lopez baking?

a. What is
b. What do
c. Are they
d. What are

**9.** _____ the news every day?

   a. Does he watch

   b. Does he watches

   c. Is he watches

   d. Is he watch

**10.** _____ ski?

   a. Do you like

   b. Does he liking to

   c. Do they like to

   d. You do like to

## CHOOSE

*Example:*

_____ calls _____ every Sunday afternoon.

   a. They . . . me

   b. Her . . . she

   c. She . . . her

   d. We . . . her

**11.** _____ talking about _____ grandchildren.

   a. Their . . . their

   b. We're . . . our

   c. She . . . her

   d. He's . . . he's

**12.** _____ write to _____ cousin in Miami every week.

   a. We're . . . our

   b. She . . . her

   c. I . . . my

   d. They . . . they're

**13.** She _____ swim very well. She _____ a good swimmer.

   a. isn't . . . doesn't

   b. doesn't . . . is

   c. not . . . isn't

   d. doesn't . . . isn't

**14.** _____ coach tells _____ he's a good soccer player.

   a. His . . . him

   b. His . . . his

   c. Hers . . . her

   d. Her . . . she

**15.** _____ play tennis very often. _____ very busy.

   a. We don't . . . We don't be

   b. She doesn't . . . She

   c. We don't . . . We're

   d. We . . . We'll

## WHAT'S THE RESPONSE?

*Example:*

I'm from Brazil.

a. That interesting.
b. Really interesting.
c. That's interesting.
d. That's interested.

**16.** Are you busy?

a. Yes, I am.
b. Yes, I do.
c. Yes. I'm.
d. No, I not.

**17.** Is Helen cleaning her attic today?

a. No, she's isn't.
b. Yes, she does.
c. Yes, she's.
d. Yes, she is.

**18.** Who are they calling?

a. Every weekend.
b. Their cousins.
c. No, they aren't.
d. Because they miss them.

**19.** Do you like to play the violin?

a. No, I'm not.
b. No, I don't.
c. No, you don't.
d. No, I don't like.

**20.** How often do you see them?

a. Three times month.
b. Twice week.
c. Once a month.
d. Once times a day.

## WHICH WORD?

You like    Do like you    Do you like    to swim? My sister Katie

is    does    do    <sup>21</sup>, and she's a very good swimmer. She practices

all time    right now    all the time    <sup>22</sup> because she    likes    wants    can    <sup>23</sup> to be

a professional swimmer when she grows up. My sister Katie's coach

tells her she    tell everybody she    says she's    <sup>24</sup> swims better than anyone else in the

school, and everyone    tells she    say she    says she's    <sup>25</sup> an excellent swimmer.

**Score:** _____

Student's Name _____  I.D. Number _____

Course _____  Teacher _____  Date _____

## CHOOSE

*Example:*

What language _____?

(a.) did he speak
b.  he spoke
c.  did he spoke
d.  was he speak

**1.** What kind of car _____?

a.  did they bought
b.  did they buy
c.  they bought
d.  bought they

**2.** _____ many pictures?

a.  Did you took
b.  What did you take
c.  Why you took so
d.  Did you take

**3.** _____ yesterday?

a.  What you did
b.  What did you did
c.  What did you do
d.  What you did do

**4.** _____ her leg?

a.  How she broke
b.  How did she broke
c.  How she did break
d.  How did she break

**5.** What happened _____?

a.  while he was skiing
b.  while was he skiing
c.  when did he ski
d.  while was he skied

## WHAT'S THE REASON?

*Example:*

Alice didn't sleep well last night
because _____.

a.  she didn't be tired
(b.) she wasn't tired
c.  she isn't tired
d.  she was tired

**6.** _____ their lines in the play because
they were nervous.

a.  They didn't forget
b.  They forget
c.  They forgetted
d.  They forgot

**7.** She didn't take the plane because _____ on time.

   a. she wasn't

   b. she didn't

   c. she's

   d. she was

**8.** I didn't drink my milk because _____.

   a. I wasn't full

   b. I wasn't thirsty

   c. was I thirsty

   d. I was thirsty

**9.** He fell asleep during the movie _____.

   a. while he was boring

   b. because it was bored

   c. because he was bored

   d. while he was bored

**10.** Stuart and Brian burned themselves because _____.

   a. they were careful

   b. they weren't careful

   c. they didn't be careful

   d. they weren't careless

## WHAT'S THE RESPONSE?

*Example:*

Did you do well on the test?

   a. Yes, I did. I wasn't prepared.

   (b.) Yes, I did. I was prepared.

   c. No, I wasn't. I prepared.

   d. No, I didn't. I was prepared.

**11.** Did she come home by boat?

   a. Yes, she did. She took a plane.

   b. No, she didn't. She came home by boat.

   c. Yes, she did. She didn't take a plane.

   d. Yes, she did. She didn't come home by boat.

**12.** Were you scared during the movie?

   a. No, I wasn't. I covered my eyes.

   b. Yes, I was. I didn't cover my eyes.

   c. No, I wasn't. I covered my eyes.

   d. Yes, I was. I covered my eyes.

**13.** Were they sad?

   a. Yes, they were. They cried.

   b. No, they weren't. They were sad.

   c. No, they weren't. They cried.

   d. Yes, they were. They didn't cry.

**14.** Did he shout at his neighbor?

   a. No, he didn't. He was angry.

   b. Yes, he did. He wasn't angry.

   c. Yes, he did. He was angry.

   d. No, he did. He wasn't angry.

**15.** Did you finish your dinner?

   a. No, we did. We weren't full.

   b. No, we didn't. We were full.

   c. No, we weren't. We didn't finish it.

   d. Yes, we were. We finished it.

## CHOOSE

*Example:*

He got into a fight with the _____ around the corner.

a. kind
(b.) kid
c. trick
d. block

**16.** I sprained my _____.

a. wallet
b. pants
c. ankle
d. shoe

**17.** She poked herself in the _____.

a. throat
b. leg
c. arm
d. eye

**18.** They were hiking in the _____.

a. bus
b. woods
c. attic
d. pool

**19.** What a shame! They _____ and fell.

a. broke
b. chopped
c. tripped
d. spilled

**20.** He ripped his _____.

a. cell phone
b. jeans
c. bicycle
d. computer

## WHAT'S THE WORD?

| play | didn't | was | played | talking | wasn't |
|------|--------|-----|--------|---------|--------|

A. You know . . . Peter didn't _____play_____ the piano very well at his concert last night.

B. He _____ **21**?

A. No. In fact, he _____ **22** very badly.

B. That's too bad! What happened?

A. While he _____ **23** playing, a man in the audience was _____ **24** on his cell phone.

B. I bet that was difficult for Peter.

A. Yes. He _____ **25** very happy.

Score: _____

| Student's Name | | I.D. Number |
| --- | --- | --- |
| Course | Teacher | Date |

## CHOOSE

*Example:*

He's _____ to work in his garden this afternoon.

a. going
b. will
c. won't
d. wants

1. _____ Larry go to the store soon?

   a. Is
   b. Will
   c. Is going
   d. Will be

2. Sarah and Henry _____ to play tennis this Friday.

   a. are going to
   b. will
   c. won't
   d. are going

3. _____ be in the office tomorrow or Wednesday.

   a. I'm not
   b. I won't
   c. I'm not going
   d. I'll won't

4. Marilyn will probably _____ on the phone for another few minutes.

   a. be talk
   b. call
   c. be talking
   d. talking

5. We _____ going to go ice skating next weekend.

   a. aren't
   b. won't
   c. can't
   d. will definitely

6. They _____ browsing the web for a long time.

   a. will probably be
   b. will
   c. are going to
   d. won't

7. Dad is going _____ muffins for breakfast this morning.

   a. have to
   b. bake
   c. to have
   d. having

8. Timothy _____ looking forward to his vacation this year.

   a. going to be
   b. is
   c. will
   d. is going to

9. Amy _____ enjoy the movie last night.

   a. wasn't
   b. won't
   c. isn't
   d. didn't

10. Andrea will be _____ her old apartment next week.

   a. leaving
   b. leave
   c. to leave
   d. going to leave

## CHOOSE

*Example:*

It won't snow until _____.

   a. last winter
   b. in the spring
   c. next winter
   d. yesterday

11. Can you call back _____?

   a. a little later
   b. last night
   c. for several hours
   d. until noon

12. _____ for a long time.

   a. She'll return
   b. She won't return
   c. She was returning
   d. Will she return

13. It'll arrive _____.

   a. until next week
   b. for a few hours
   c. last night
   d. in a few minutes

14. James is studying very hard _____.

   a. a little later
   b. tonight
   c. last semester
   d. next weekend

15. My wife's train will arrive at _____.

   a. eight o'clock
   b. a long time
   c. later this morning
   d. a few minutes

## WHOSE IS IT?

*Example:*

I'm sure he'll be happy to lend you _____.

   a. him
   b. his
   c. he's
   d. their

16. Are these dictionaries _____?

   a. our
   b. ours
   c. your
   d. them

**17.** Could I possibly borrow _____ hammer?

    a. yours

    b. you're

    c. your husbands

    d. your

**18.** _____ be happy to lend you a screwdriver.

    a. They'll

    b. Their

    c. There

    d. You'll

**19.** I finished my composition, but my sister didn't finish _____.

    a. her

    b. her's

    c. mine

    d. hers

**20.** If you don't have a pencil, you can use _____.

    a. me

    b. our

    c. mine

    d. my

## WHICH WORD?

A. Hi. This | (is)   will be   I'm | Angela. Can you talk for a minute?

B. I'm sorry. I can't talk | soon   now   then |²¹. I'm paying my bills.

Can you call back later?

A. Sure. How much longer | are   going to   will |²² you be

paying your bills?

B. Probably | in   for   at |²³ another | minutes   while   hour |²⁴.

A. Okay. I'll call back a little | late   later   while |²⁵.

**Score:** _____

| | |
|---|---|
| Student's Name _____ | I.D. Number _____ |
| Course _____ Teacher _____ | Date _____ |

## CHOOSE

*Example:*

My brother and I _____ horses for many years.

- (a.) have ridden
- b. are riding
- c. are ridden
- d. haven't rode

**1.** Nancy and Steve _____ a movie in a long time.

- a. have seen
- b. haven't seen
- c. hasn't seen
- d. aren't seeing

**2.** _____ to the bank yet?

- a. You went
- b. Did you gone
- c. Have you went
- d. Have you gone

**3.** _____ in the hospital last year.

- a. I've been
- b. I haven't been
- c. I was
- d. I been

**4.** He's _____ in an airplane.

- a. never flying
- b. never flown
- c. flew yet
- d. flown yet

**5.** _____ reports for many years.

- a. I've written
- b. I write
- c. I've wrote
- d. I'm not writing

**6.** _____ scuba diving last year.

- a. I've gone
- b. I haven't gone
- c. I went
- d. Have you gone

**7.** Sue has _____ well in school this year.

- a. didn't done
- b. not did
- c. did
- d. done

**8.** Ted _____ a suit in a long time.

- a. didn't wear
- b. hasn't worn
- c. isn't wearing
- d. has worn

**9.** _____ inventory a little while ago.
   a. We took
   b. We're taking
   c. We've taken
   d. We haven't taken

**10.** He _____ his medicine now.
   a. has taken
   b. hasn't taken
   c. has took
   d. has to take

## CHOOSE

*Example:*

  A. Has your son Ricky gone to bed yet?
  B. No, he _____.
    a. didn't
    (b.) hasn't
    c. isn't
    d. haven't

**11.** A. Why hasn't Rita finished her report?
    B. She _____ had the time.
    a. doesn't
    b. haven't
    c. hasn't
    d. didn't

**12.** A. Has Charlie bought apples this week?
    B. No. He _____ apples last week.
    a. has bought
    b. bought
    c. didn't buy
    d. hasn't bought

**13.** A. Why isn't Helen going to do her laundry today?
    B. _____ it this week.
    a. She already done
    b. She's already did
    c. She hasn't done
    d. She's already done

**14.** A. Have you ever been in the hospital?
    B. _____.
    a. Yes, I've been.
    b. Yes, I was.
    c. Yes, you have.
    d. No, I haven't.

**15.** A. Have your parents met your new teacher yet?
    B. No. _____ met her yet.
    a. They didn't
    b. They haven't
    c. They don't want to
    d. They've

## CHOOSE

*Example:*

Frank hasn't _____ gotten a raise.

   a. a long time
   b. never
   (c.) ever
   d. now

16. Marty has drawn cartoons _____.

   a. for a long time
   b. last summer
   c. in a long time
   d. all yesterday afternoon

17. Maria gave an excellent speech _____.

   a. now
   b. yesterday evening
   c. yet
   d. next weekend

18. Betsy and Bob have _____ eaten with chopsticks.

   a. never
   b. ever
   c. yet
   d. wanted to

19. Jimmy fell asleep in class _____.

   a. in a long time
   b. now
   c. already
   d. this morning

20. Have you gone kayaking _____?

   a. ever
   b. right now
   c. yet
   d. in a long time

## WHAT'S THE WORD?

| haven't | hasn't | yet | already | have | wasn't |
|---------|--------|-----|---------|------|--------|

A. I see you haven't gone home _____ yet _____.

B. No. I _____ [21] finished typing an important letter. My computer

   _____ [22] working well today. It _____ [23] worked well all week.

A. That's too bad. Well, do you want to _____ [24] dinner together after work?

B. No, thanks. I've _____ [25] eaten dinner.

A. Okay. Have a nice weekend.

B. You, too.

Score: _____

Student's Name _____ I.D. Number _____

Course _____ Teacher _____ Date _____

## CHOOSE

*Example:*

We've known each other _____ two months.

(a.) for
b. since

**1.** Paula has studied Spanish _____ the past few years.

a. for
b. since

**2.** Jim has owned a car _____ 2002.

a. for
b. since

**3.** Mr. Wong has been in this country _____ he finished college.

a. for
b. since

**4.** Mike and Elaine have had a dog _____ a year.

a. for
b. since

**5.** I've been sick _____ last week.

a. for
b. since

## CHOOSE

*Example:*

Paul _____ the piano since he was five.

a. plays
(b.) has played
c. is playing
d. didn't play

**6.** Diane _____ the cello every day at three o'clock.

a. practices
b. is practicing
c. hasn't practiced
d. has practice

**7.** Alexander, how long _____ in college?

a. are you
b. you been
c. have you been
d. you be

**8.** Susan _____ classical music for a long time.

a. is liking
b. likes
c. doesn't like
d. has liked

**9.** _____ how to swim?

    a. How long did you know

    b. Do you know

    c. How long have you know

    d. How long have you've known

**10.** Steve _____ in New York since last summer.

    a. is living

    b. lived

    c. lives

    d. has lived

## CHOOSE

*Example:*

_____ at Sam's Supermarket for a while?

    a. Did you worked

    (b.) Have you worked

    c. Do you work

    d. Have you've worked

**11.** Victor _____ an engineer for a long time.

    a. been

    b. is

    c. has to want to be

    d. has wanted to be

**12.** When _____ the manager?

    a. have you become

    b. did you become

    c. did you became

    d. have you've become

**13.** Alice _____ to Los Angeles in 2003.

    a. has moved

    b. hasn't moved

    c. moved

    d. have moved

**14.** I've been a science teacher for two years. Before that, _____ a math teacher.

    a. I've been

    b. I was

    c. I'm

    d. I haven't been

**15.** Carla _____ to a movie in a long time.

    a. hasn't gone

    b. didn't go

    c. went

    d. isn't going

## CHOOSE

*Example:*

Jonathan _____ from college two years ago.

    a. has graduated

    (b.) graduated

    c. graduates

    d. will graduate

**16.** Mr. and Mrs. Evans _____ two car accidents recently.

    a. have

    b. have had

    c. are having

    d. have to have

**17.** My daughter _____ interested in computers since she was a teenager.

  a. is

  b. was

  c. has been

  d. been

**18.** How long _____ Gail been a doctor?

  a. did

  b. has

  c. have

  d. is

**19.** William _____ skim milk all his life.

  a. has drunk

  b. drinks

  c. is drinking

  d. has drank

**20.** Mario _____ a taxi driver for a few years. Before that, he was a barber.

  a. been

  b. has

  c. is

  d. has been

## WHAT'S THE WORD?

| since | for | haven't | didn't | don't | seen |
|-------|-----|---------|--------|-------|------|

A. Hi, Henry. I haven't _____*seen*_____ you at the office _____ <sup>21</sup> a few days.

How have you been?

B. As a matter of fact, I've been sick _____ <sup>22</sup> last Thursday.

A. Oh. I _____ <sup>23</sup> know that.

B. I think I got sick because I _____ <sup>24</sup> eaten any healthy food in a long time,

and I _____ <sup>25</sup> exercise.

A. I see. Well, I hope you feel better soon.

**Score: _____**

Student's Name _____  I.D. Number _____

Course _____  Teacher _____  Date _____

## CHOOSE

*Example:*

A. Will Professor Bennett return soon?
B. No. She won't return _____ several hours.
   a. until
   (b.) for
   c. in
   d. since

1. A. How long has Eric studied French?
B. He's studied French _____ he was in high school.
   a. for
   b. until
   c. since
   d. because

2. A. Diane hurt herself while she _____ off a bus.
B. That's a shame.
   a. was getting
   b. gets
   c. has gotten
   d. is getting

3. A. How often _____ Laura compose poetry?
B. Every few weeks.
   a. has
   b. does
   c. was
   d. is

4. A. Could you please give me _____ car keys?
B. Yes, of course.
   a. ours
   b. you're
   c. yours
   d. your

5. A. Are these your books?
B. No. They're _____.
   a. theirs
   b. them
   c. their
   d. mine

6. A. _____ do you and Larry go camping?
B. About twice a year.
   a. How
   b. Where
   c. How often
   d. Why

7. A. Do Bob and his wife own their own house?
B. Yes. They've owned their own house _____ several years.
   a. since
   b. because
   c. until
   d. for

8. A. Janet _____ this morning.
   B. I'm surprised to hear that. She hasn't swum in a long time.
      a. has swum
      b. swam
      c. swum
      d. hasn't swum

9. A. Can you come to _____ party this Saturday night?
   B. Yes. I'll be there.
      a. mine
      b. ours
      c. our
      d. are

10. A. _____ to the bank yet?
    B. Yes. I went to the bank an hour ago.
       a. Have you gone
       b. Are you going
       c. Can you go
       d. Will you go

11. A. Why was Gary disappointed?
    B. He _____ very well this morning.
       a. wasn't teaching
       b. didn't teach
       c. hasn't taught
       d. taught

12. A. Is Maria sick?
    B. Yes. _____ sick for more than a week.
       a. She's
       b. She was
       c. She's been
       d. Will she be

13. A. Did you like the movie?
    B. Yes. It's one of the best movies _____.
       a. I've ever saw
       b. I've ever seen
       c. I've seen yet
       d. I've already saw

14. A. _____ Alice be able to come to our party next week?
    B. Yes. I think so.
       a. Can
       b. Maybe
       c. Do you think
       d. Will

15. A. I've _____ done the laundry.
    B. When did you do it?
       a. already
       b. ever
       c. never
       d. yet

16. A. Is Kim busy?
    B. Yes. She's _____ cookies.
       a. bakes
       b. baked
       c. baking
       d. been baked

17. A. _____ you taken the dog for a walk?
    B. Yes. I did that an hour ago.
       a. Have
       b. Can
       c. Did
       d. Will

**18.** A. Nancy and I _____ the lottery yet.
B. I'm sure you will someday.

    a. have won

    b. haven't won

    c. aren't winning

    d. won

**19.** A. Who _____ the students talking about the other day?
B. I'm not sure.

    a. are

    b. have been

    c. were

    d. will

**20.** A. Is this Jerry's notebook?
B. No. It's _____.

    a. our

    b. mine

    c. my

    d. their

## CHOOSE

*Example:*

I have a lot of homework. I'll probably _____ all evening.

    a. will study

    (b.) be studying

    c. will be studying

    d. won't study

**21.** What _____ yesterday afternoon?

    a. you read

    b. have you read

    c. were you reading

    d. are you reading

**22.** What kind of car _____ Ms. Jackson _____ this afternoon?

    a. does . . . buy

    b. has . . . bought

    c. did . . . buy

    d. will . . . buying

**23.** Bruce _____ probably going to practice football this afternoon.

    a. is

    b. will

    c. might

    d. won't

**24.** Carla _____ seventeen e-mail messages this morning.

    a. is writing

    b. writes

    c. has wrote

    d. has written

**25.** I'll call you sometime _____ week.

    a. next

    b. last

    c. in a

    d. until a

**26.** Hector _____ been in a helicopter.

   a. hasn't never

   b. has never

   c. isn't ever

   d. isn't yet

**27.** Susan _____ overtime last week.

   a. has worked

   b. hasn't worked

   c. works

   d. worked

**28.** I'll probably _____ a taxi for another few years.

   a. have driven

   b. will drive

   c. be going to drive

   d. be driving

**29.** Joe owned a restaurant _____.

   a. since 2001

   b. for 2002

   c. between 1999 and 2003

   d. until next year

**30.** Mrs. Jenkins _____ our English teacher for the past year.

   a. was

   b. has been

   c. is

   d. is been

**31.** Michelle _____ to music when the phone rang.

   a. listens

   b. will be listening

   c. has listened

   d. was listening

**32.** Linda is an actress, but she _____ on TV yet.

   a. didn't go

   b. wasn't

   c. hasn't been

   d. has been

**33.** Brian _____ while it _____ today.

   a. has hiked . . . was raining

   b. was hiking . . . was raining

   c. is hiking . . . is raining

   d. doesn't hike . . . will be raining

**34.** _____ you go scuba diving?

   a. When did

   b. How often have

   c. Where have

   d. When will you

**35.** How long _____ interested in Chinese history?

   a. are you

   b. have you been

   c. did you be

   d. you are

**36.** Jimmy _____ his car a week ago.

   a. washes

   b. will be washing

   c. has washed

   d. washed

**37.** Tina _____ really looking forward to her vacation this year.

   a. has

   b. will

   c. is

   d. not

**38.** Louis _____ to a concert in a long time.

    a. hasn't gone

    b. didn't go

    c. has gone

    d. won't go

**39.** Mabel hasn't taken her medicine yet. She _____ it now.

    a. has taken

    b. has to take

    c. taking

    d. already took

**40.** They won't see each other _____ next year.

    a. for

    b. since

    c. until

    d. for

## WHICH WORD?

Carlos [ has wanted (wanted) wants ] to go skiing last weekend, but he injured

[ him hisself himself ] **41** while he [ has hiked was hiking hiked ] **42** in

the woods. [ For By Since ] **43** then, he [ is was has been ] **44** very bored

because he has to stay in his room. He has [ yet already still ] **45** read several

books, watched TV, and written some letters, but he still [ was be feels ] **46** bored.

He's [ going looking thinking ] **47** forward to this afternoon. Some of his friends

[ will will be are going ] **48** visit him, but none of them

[ call calling have called ] **49** him yet. Luckily, the doctor says he'll feel better

[ until in for ] **50** a few days.

Score: _____

Student's Name _____ I.D. Number _____

Course _____ Teacher _____ Date _____

## CHOOSE

*Example:*

  A. What have you been doing?
  B. _____ pictures all day.

    a. I'm drawing
    (b.) I've been drawing
    c. I drew
    d. I drawn

**1.** A. Where are your neighbors going for their vacation?
  B. I think _____ to Hawaii.

    a. they've been going
    b. they go
    c. they're going
    d. they've been gone

**2.** A. How long has Denise been doing sit-ups?
  B. _____ for a half hour.

    a. She's doing them
    b. She did them
    c. They've been doing her
    d. She's been doing them

**3.** A. How many notes have you written?
  B. _____ more than fifty.

    a. I'm already writing
    b. I've already written
    c. I'm already writing
    d. I've already been written

**4.** A. Have we been in line for a long time?
  B. No. _____ here for only ten minutes.

    a. We're
    b. We've been standing
    c. We stood
    d. We're standing

**5.** A. How long did Carl work at the post office?
  B. _____ there for thirty years.

    a. He's been working
    b. He's worked
    c. He's working
    d. He worked

## CHOOSE

*Example:*

Mario is exhausted. _____ pizzas since ten o'clock.

  a. He's making
  (b.) He's been making
  c. He made
  d. He'll make

**6.** Sally is frustrated. She _____ her keys for hours.

  a. has been looking for
  b. is looking for
  c. looks for
  d. has been looked for

7. My sisters and I _____ in the marathon next weekend.

   a. have been running
   b. are going to run
   c. have run
   d. didn't run

8. That police officer _____ already _____ traffic for seven hours today.

   a. has . . . directing
   b. has been . . . directed
   c. has . . . directed
   d. is . . . directing

9. Victor _____ photographs since nine o'clock this morning.

   a. is taking
   b. already takes
   c. has already taken
   d. has been taking

10. Thelma has never _____ to so many job interviews in one week before.

   a. went
   b. gone
   c. go
   d. been going

## CHOOSE

*Example:*

Our roof has been leaking for _____.

   (a.) two days
   b. this morning
   c. today
   d. yesterday morning

11. The phone has been ringing _____.

   a. yesterday
   b. all night
   c. a few minutes ago
   d. nine o'clock

12. I've _____ eaten a lot of apples today.

   a. never
   b. already
   c. been
   d. still

13. It's been raining for _____.

   a. a week
   b. all day
   c. an hour ago
   d. yesterday afternoon

14. We've been waiting since _____.

   a. a few hours
   b. 9:30
   c. fifteen minutes
   d. half an hour

15. My cousins haven't written to me for _____.

   a. only last week
   b. last month
   c. a long time
   d. I moved to Chicago

16. I haven't met anyone interesting since _____.

   a. a long time
   b. all year
   c. many years
   d. I graduated from college

**17.** Rick hasn't practiced the guitar _____.

    a. all week

    b. a week

    c. a week ago

    d. yesterday morning

**18.** Jane _____ hasn't gone to the doctor.

    a. already

    b. never

    c. yet

    d. still

**19.** Have they been working _____ night?

    a. all

    b. last

    c. tomorrow

    d. yesterday

**20.** Gary has been exercising for _____ an hour.

    a. more

    b. about

    c. already

    d. before

## WHICH WORD?

**A.** I've been feeling [ (nervous)    furious    angry ] recently.

I've [ never riding    ever ridden    never ridden ]²¹ on a motorcycle, and I'm going

to ride on one [ tomorrow    before    about an hour ]²² .

**B.** Don't be nervous. I've [ been ridden    been riding    riding ]²³ on motorcycles for many

years.

**A.** Really? [ Did    Were    Have ]²⁴ you ever [ been    be    being ]²⁵ in an

accident?

**B.** No. Never.

**Score:** _____

Student's Name _____ I.D. Number _____

Course _____ Teacher _____ Date _____

## CHOOSE

*Example:*

Does your sister _____ to play tennis?

a. practice
b. enjoy
c. like  *(circled)*
d. think about

**1.** Timothy usually avoids _____ at fast-food restaurants.

a. to eat
b. eat
c. going
d. eating

**2.** Your son _____ going to bed earlier.

a. doesn't like to
b. should start
c. has always hating
d. should decide

**3.** I've been _____ to do karate since I was ten years old.

a. keeping on
b. thinking
c. learning
d. considering

**4.** James and Margaret don't _____ standing in line.

a. like to
b. decide
c. can't stand
d. enjoy

**5.** Our dog _____ sleeping all the time.

a. likes to
b. keeps on
c. been
d. quits

## CHOOSE

*Example:*

She's _____ eating too much junk food.

a. keeps on
b. been  *(circled)*
c. doesn't enjoy
d. continues

**6.** Have you ever tried _____ your nails before?

a. to quit to bite
b. to bite to quit
c. quit to bite
d. to quit biting

**7.** Jane _____ moving to New York.

    a. decided

    b. can't stood

    c. considered

    d. has thought

**8.** How long have you been _____ going on a diet?

    a. deciding

    b. avoiding

    c. thinking

    d. to consider

**9.** You can't _____ for the rest of your life.

    a. keep on to complain

    b. to continue to complain

    c. continue complaining

    d. complaining

**10.** Why did you _____ wearing a tie and jacket when you were young?

    a. learn

    b. hate

    c. decide

    d. start to

## CHOOSE

*Example:*

I've decided _____ teasing my little brother.

    (a.) to stop

    b. stopping

    c. stop

    d. stopping to

**11.** I think _____ on a diet is a great idea.

    a. go

    b. going

    c. be

    d. gone

**12.** I'm thinking about _____ married.

    a. getting

    b. to get

    c. been

    d. get

**13.** How long have you _____ a piano?

    a. been thinking to buy

    b. thought to buy

    c. considering buying

    d. been thinking of buying

**14.** Kathy loves her cell phone. That's why she can't stop _____ it.

    a. to use

    b. using

    c. use

    d. to like

**15.** _____ people is very rude.

    a. Interrupt

    b. Avoid saying hello to

    c. Interrupting

    d. Talk about

## CHOOSE

*Example:*

I've never been _____ before.

a. swum
b. to swim
c. swimming
d. be swimming

**16.** Albert _____ to travel to Europe by plane next week.

a. is going
b. will be
c. is thinking
d. might consider

**17.** George _____ his exercises in a long time.

a. didn't do
b. hasn't done
c. has been doing
d. has been thinking about doing

**18.** _____ very difficult?

a. Doesn't surfing be
b. Isn't surfing
c. Does surfing be
d. To surf is

**19.** Susie _____ her room since ten o'clock this morning.

a. has cleaned
b. was cleaning
c. is cleaning
d. has been cleaning

**20.** Do you think _____ a vegetarian is healthy?

a. be
b. been
c. being
d. have been

## WHAT'S THE WORD?

| to do | working | starting | to quit | doing | to go |

A. Guess what I've decided _____*to do*_____!

B. What?

A. I've decided _____<sup>21</sup> my job.

B. Really? Why?

A. I can't stand _____<sup>22</sup> at my company.  I don't think I can stand

_____<sup>23</sup> there every day.

B. What are you going to do?

A. I've been considering _____<sup>24</sup> my own business.

B. That's great!  How long have you been thinking about _____<sup>25</sup> that?

A. For a long time, actually.

B. Well, I hope you're successful.

**Score:** _____

Student's Name _____ I.D. Number _____

Course _____ Teacher _____ Date _____

## CHOOSE

*Example:*

A. Why didn't your parents go to the movies last night?
B. They _____ a movie the night before.
   a. didn't see
   b. had been seeing
   c. had seen
   d. have seen

1. A. What was Mrs. Lee doing in her garden this morning?
   B. She _____ her plants.
   a. was watering
   b. had been watering
   c. had watered
   d. has watered

2. A. Why was Albert so tired last night?
   B. _____ all day.
   a. He's been skiing
   b. He's skied
   c. He had skied
   d. He's skiing

3. A. Did Helen enjoy discussing politics last night?
   B. Yes. She _____ politics in a long time.
   a. hadn't been discussed
   b. had discussed
   c. didn't discuss
   d. hadn't discussed

4. A. Has Pamela ever been to Paris?
   B. Yes. She _____ there last year.
   a. had gone
   b. went
   c. has gone
   d. had been going

5. A. Why did Sam have trouble flying a kite last weekend?
   B. _____ never flown one before.
   a. He had
   b. He
   c. He hadn't
   d. He's

## CHOOSE

*Example:*

By the time I got there, the game _____.
   a. had already started
   b. started
   c. had been starting
   d. has started

6. Harry's wife had already finished eating dinner when he _____ home.
   a. had come
   b. was coming
   c. came
   d. has come

7. James _____ that his shirt was dirty until after dinner.

   a. realized
   b. hadn't realized
   c. hasn't realized
   d. wasn't realizing

8. Jane _____ for just a few minutes before she got tired.

   a. had been swimming
   b. has swum
   c. is swimming
   d. has been swimming

9. Jeffrey has a job interview today. He _____ his shoes for an hour.

   a. had been shining
   b. is shining
   c. shines
   d. has been shining

10. How long _____ for your dinner party last weekend?

   a. had you prepared
   b. hadn't you been preparing
   c. have you been preparing
   d. you prepared

## CHOOSE

*Example:*

Mona hadn't _____ in a long time.

   a. thought about
   (b.) gone fishing
   c. brought along
   d. deserved

11. By the time I got there, the boat had _____.

   a. taken off
   b. begun
   c. sailed away
   d. ended

12. Jim had been _____ for the concert for a long time.

   a. rehearsing
   b. wrestling
   c. realizing
   d. performing

13. She really _____ to win the race.

   a. described
   b. discussed
   c. dislocated
   d. deserved

14. Roger hadn't _____ to lock his front door.

   a. believed
   b. memorized
   c. remembered
   d. felt

15. I hadn't _____ through that park in a year.

   a. fallen
   b. walked
   c. brought
   d. caught

## WHICH WORD DOESN'T BELONG?

*Example:*

a. go canoeing    (b.) water plants    c. see a movie    d. fly a kite

**16.** a. practice    b. train    c. rehearse    d. perform

**17.** a. swim    b. play the guitar    c. do gymnastics    d. wrestle

**18.** a. forget    b. memorize    c. remember    d. learn

**19.** a. prepare    b. plan    c. fall through    d. get ready

**20.** a. lose    b. sprain    c. twist    d. break

## WHICH WORD?

A. Have you heard about Jennifer and Jack?

B. No, I | didn't    hadn't    (haven't) | . What

| had happened    is happened    happened |²¹ ?

A. They | had broken    broke    were breaking |²² up last weekend.

B. That's too bad. Why did they break up?

A. Jennifer got a job in London, and she decided | taking    take to    to take |²³ it.

B. That's a shame. They | weren't    had been    been |²⁴ going out for a long time.

A. Yes . . . and someone told me they had even

| been thinking    considered    decided |²⁵ about getting married.

**Score:** _____

| Student's Name _____ | I.D. Number _____ |
| Course _____ Teacher _____ | Date _____ |

## CHOOSE

*Example:*

I didn't drink the old milk in the refrigerator. I _____ it out.

- (a.) threw
- b. filled
- c. crossed
- d. turned

**1.** It's late, and Dave is still sleeping. We need to _____ him up.

- a. take
- b. use
- c. wake
- d. put

**2.** It's cold in here. Could you _____ the heat on?

- a. call
- b. turn
- c. try
- d. give

**3.** Howard forgot my phone number because he hadn't _____ it down.

- a. done
- b. turned
- c. filled
- d. written

**4.** Lucy _____ off her husband at the train station this morning.

- a. ran
- b. dropped
- c. took
- d. threw

**5.** Has Peter _____ up his new computer yet?

- a. used
- b. looked
- c. hooked
- d. hung

## CHOOSE

*Example:*

A. What does this word mean?
B. You should _____ in a dictionary.

- a. do it over
- (b.) look it up
- c. write it down
- d. pick it out

**6.** A. Do you like this sweater?
B. Yes. I think you should _____.

- a. try it on
- b. bring it back
- c. get along with it
- d. put it away

7.  A.  Is Harry finished with the
        newspaper?
    B.  Yes.  He should _____.

        a.  put it on
        b.  throw it away
        c.  look it through
        d.  take it off

8.  A.  Has Sally read these library books?
    B.  Yes.  She should _____ to the library.

        a.  take after them
        b.  put them away
        c.  take them back
        d.  throw them away

9.  A.  Have you seen my glasses?
    B.  No.  You should _____ them in
        your room.

        a.  run into
        b.  look up
        c.  put on
        d.  look for

10. A.  Has Johnny finished his homework?
    B.  Yes.  He's going to _____ now.

        a.  hand it in
        b.  figure it out
        c.  get over it
        d.  turn it on

## CHOOSE

*Example:*

Gloria's children definitely take

_____.

(a.) after her
b.  her after
c.  them after
d.  on them

11. Brian moved to Chicago last month.
    Has anybody _____?

    a.  heard him from
    b.  heard from him
    c.  heard from
    d.  heard him

12. I don't think they _____ carefully.

    a.  thought it over
    b.  think it over
    c.  thought over it
    d.  think over it

13. Larry found the answer when he

    _____.

    a.  looked his textbook through
    b.  looked through his textbook
    c.  looked them through
    d.  looked it through

14. The garbage is in the kitchen.  Could
    you please _____?

    a.  take out it
    b.  take out them
    c.  take them out
    d.  take it out

15. Peggy hadn't seen her uncle for a long
    time.  She was glad she _____ yesterday.

    a.  ran into him
    b.  ran him into
    c.  ran into her
    d.  ran her into

## CHOOSE

*Example:*

Has she ever taken anything
_____ to a store?

(a.) back
b. on
c. down
d. off

**16.** Kevin should consider doing his
college application form _____.

a. off
b. up
c. back
d. over

**17.** Vicky left her coat _____ because she
was still cold.

a. off
b. up
c. on
d. away

**18.** Why doesn't Billy get along _____ his
sister?

a. with
b. after
c. back
d. to

**19.** Ms. Smith never calls _____ me during
class.

a. up
b. out of
c. on
d. over

**20.** Abigail needs to clean _____ her
room.

a. through
b. back
c. off
d. up

## WHAT'S THE WORD?

| called up | take down | come over | hung up | run out of | put |
|-----------|-----------|-----------|---------|------------|-----|

There was a big party at my house last night.  I _____*called up*_____ all of my friends

and asked them to _____ **21**. My wife and I made lots of things to eat and drink,

and we _____ **22** decorations everywhere.  We were lucky.  We had bought a lot of

food, so we didn't _____ **23** anything.  Today I have a lot to do.  I have to

_____ **24** all the decorations and _____ **25** them away.

**Score:** _____

## CHOOSE

*Example:*

> My older sister can swim very well, but _____.
>
> a. I can, too
> b. neither can I
> c. I can't
> d. I can't either

**1.** Your brother shouldn't do that, and you _____.

a. shouldn't either
b. don't either
c. don't
d. shouldn't neither

**2.** That man wants this job, and _____.

a. either does she
b. does she, too
c. so does she
d. so she does

**3.** We don't walk our dog every morning, but _____.

a. our neighbors do
b. neither don't our neighbors
c. our neighbors don't, too
d. our neighbors don't either

**4.** You and Vanessa aren't in a theater group, and _____.

a. I don't either
b. neither do I
c. I'm not
d. I'm not either

**5.** She's already eaten, and _____.

a. neither has he
b. so has he
c. so is he
d. he hasn't either

## CHOOSE

*Example:*

> I go on a lot of business trips, _____ does my husband.
>
> a. and
> b. but
> c. but neither
> d. and so

**6.** Rita can't play the piano very well, _____ can her sister.

a. and so
b. but so
c. and neither
d. but

**7.** Henry and I didn't do well on the exam, _____.

    a. but neither has Susan

    b. but Susan did

    c. and so did Susan

    d. and didn't Susan either

**8.** Jimmy hasn't seen a movie in a long time, and Judy _____.

    a. has, too

    b. has neither

    c. has either

    d. hasn't either

**9.** Harold couldn't walk his dog when he was sick, but his wife _____.

    a. could either

    b. didn't

    c. could

    d. couldn't

**10.** Debbie wasn't discouraged, _____ her husband was.

    a. and neither

    b. but so

    c. and so

    d. but

## CHOOSE

*Example:*

John _____ skate very well, and Jane _____ either.

    a. doesn't . . . does

    b. shouldn't . . . should

    c. can't . . . can't

    d. can . . . can

**11.** Emma _____ majored in chemistry, but Steven _____.

    a. had . . . had

    b. didn't . . . did

    c. hadn't . . . had

    d. hasn't . . . hasn't

**12.** The students in my class _____ speaking English, and _____, too.

    a. enjoy . . . I am

    b. enjoy . . . I do

    c. are learning . . . I am

    d. like . . . do I

**13.** Larry _____ for a long time, and Lucy _____ either.

    a. has been singing . . . hasn't

    b. hadn't sung . . . had

    c. has been singing . . . has

    d. hasn't been singing . . . hasn't

**14.** He _____ really be hopeful, and so _____ you.

    a. should . . . should

    b. shouldn't . . . should

    c. will . . . won't

    d. won't . . . will

**15.** Mr. Lane _____ come to the party, but his wife _____.

    a. will . . . is able to

    b. can . . . will

    c. won't . . . will

    d. is able to . . . can

## CHOOSE

*Example:*

A. Why do Sal and his sister look so frightened?
B. He's never flown in an airplane before, _____.

    a. but has she
    (b.) and neither has she
    c. but she hasn't either
    d. and so has she

16. A. I'm allergic to fish.
    B. What a coincidence! _____.

    a. Neither am I.
    b. I'm not either.
    c. So am I.
    d. I'm not, too.

17. A. Where do you and your wife want to go?
    B. I want to go to Mexico, _____.

    a. and so does she, too
    b. and so does she
    c. and so she does
    d. but she does, too

18. A. Why don't your children like fairy tales?
    B. My son thinks they're scary, _____.

    a. but my daughter doesn't either
    b. and my daughter isn't
    c. but my daughter does
    d. and my daughter does, too

19. A. Can you and Bob come to the office on Saturday?
    B. I can't, but _____.

    a. Bob can't either
    b. Bob can
    c. neither can Bob
    d. so can Bob

20. A. Why did Edgar get laid off?
    B. He _____ any special training, but his co-workers had.

    a. hadn't had
    b. didn't have
    c. doesn't have
    d. hasn't had

## WHICH WORD?

Peter and his girlfriend Sarah have been going out for a long time. They like

each other very much, but they're | compatible    similar    (different) |. He's very

athletic, but she | is    isn't    doesn't |²¹. He likes to play sports, but she

| does, too    doesn't either    doesn't |²².

However, Peter and Sarah are also very | similar    willing    different |²³. Peter

can't stand loud music, | but so    and so    and neither |²⁴ can Sarah. And Peter

has a very hopeful outlook on life, and Sarah | does, too    hasn't    isn't |²⁵.

**Score:** _____

| Student's Name _____ | I.D. Number _____ |
| Course _____ Teacher _____ | Date _____ |

## CHOOSE

*Example:*

I'm going to _____ about my health.

- (a.) stop worrying
- b. quit to worry
- c. stop to worry
- d. avoid to worry

**1.** My neighbors _____ since early this morning.

- a. already argued
- b. have been arguing
- c. had argued
- d. are arguing

**2.** Alan is afraid of flying, _____ is his wife.

- a. and so
- b. but so
- c. and neither
- d. but neither

**3.** When did you _____ how to play the violin?

- a. decide learning
- b. learning
- c. decide to learn
- d. learned

**4.** She didn't want to fly a kite because she _____ one the week before.

- a. flew
- b. has flown
- c. had been flying
- d. had flown

**5.** It's ten o'clock. Why _____ you done your homework?

- a. haven't
- b. hadn't
- c. didn't
- d. aren't

**6.** Terry doesn't often _____ an invitation to a party.

- a. take down
- b. take back
- c. turn down
- d. turn off

**7.** By the time the movie ended, I _____ asleep!

- a. have fallen
- b. had fallen
- c. had been falling
- d. had fell

**8.** Natalie is really tired. She's _____ overtime all week.

- a. working
- b. been training
- c. has been working
- d. been working

**9.** Is that Dan's mother? He really takes _____.

- a. her after
- b. after her
- c. her back
- d. up to her

**10.** Betty's mother won't allow her to do that, _____.

   a. and neither will her father

   b. and so will her father

   c. and her father doesn't either

   d. but her father won't

**11.** Julio _____ for his English test for a long time, but he still did poorly.

   a. is studying

   b. has studied

   c. studied

   d. hadn't been studying

**12.** As soon as Carmen woke up, she realized that she _____ to do her laundry the day before.

   a. forgot

   b. had forgotten

   c. had been forgetting

   d. has forgotten

**13.** Why are you avoiding _____ about the problem with your teacher?

   a. talking

   b. been talking

   c. talk

   d. to talk

**14.** I'm not surprised William lost so much weight last year. _____ a lot.

   a. He's exercising

   b. He's been exercising

   c. He wasn't exercising

   d. He had been exercising

**15.** Scott _____ since he was very young.

   a. hasn't gone fishing

   b. hasn't been fished

   c. didn't go fishing

   d. isn't going fishing

**16.** Mr. and Mrs. Gomez have a nice car, _____.

   a. and so do we, too

   b. and we do, too

   c. but we don't either

   d. and so is ours

**17.** How long _____ a job opening at this company?

   a. had been

   b. is there

   c. has there been

   d. has there being

**18.** I'm sure you'll do well on the test. _____ for it for quite a long time.

   a. You had been preparing

   b. You're preparing

   c. You prepare

   d. You've been preparing

**19.** _____ to play golf takes a long time.

   a. Considering

   b. Practicing

   c. Learning

   d. Decide

**20.** Are you busy now? Would you like to _____?

   a. run into me

   b. come over

   c. get over

   d. leave on

**21.** Grandpa _____ better until the weather got cold.

   a. has been feeling

   b. has felt

   c. had been feeling

   d. feels

**22.** Why doesn't your friend Bill get
_____?

  a. along with his sister

  b. his sister along with

  c. along his sister with

  d. with his sister along

**23.** Wendy _____ doing the tango until
she took a dance class.

  a. hasn't been

  b. hadn't liked

  c. wouldn't like

  d. hasn't been liking

**24.** My wife is very liberal, but _____.

  a. I don't

  b. I am, too

  c. I'm not

  d. neither am I

**25.** Martha's landlord _____ everything in
her apartment, but mine hasn't.

  a. has fixed

  b. had fixed

  c. hasn't fixed

  d. hadn't fixed

**26.** I'm considering _____ a job in an
insurance company in Dallas.

  a. to take

  b. taking

  c. take

  d. taken

**27.** Gary had been having headaches
_____ until last Thursday.

  a. every time

  b. before

  c. last month

  d. once a day

**28.** Are we there yet? I feel like _____ all
night long.

  a. we had been driving

  b. we drive

  c. we've been driving

  d. we're driving

**29.** The neighbors had already given a
party _____.

  a. recently

  b. the weekend before

  c. until we did

  d. in a long time

**30.** It hasn't rained _____.

  a. in the past few weeks

  b. the day before

  c. a few weeks ago

  d. last week

**31.** Jim and his friends have been standing
in line for tickets _____.

  a. until more than two hours

  b. by six o'clock

  c. for today

  d. all day

**32.** Have you _____ met a famous actor or
actress?

  a. still

  b. ever

  c. yet

  d. wanted to

**33.** I want my nephew to stop biting his
nails, but he _____ doing it.

  a. learns

  b. can't stand

  c. keeps on

  d. won't

**34.** We weren't surprised when you got a raise. _____ working hard for a long time.

   a. You had been

   b. You were

   c. You hadn't been

   d. You're

**35.** Could you tell me the answers to the math questions? I couldn't figure _____.

   a. out them

   b. them out

   c. it out

   d. out it

**36.** How long _____ the cello before you became a professional?

   a. have you been playing

   b. have you played

   c. had you played

   d. are you playing

**37.** I haven't _____ in two weeks.

   a. been hearing from him

   b. been heard from him

   c. heard him from

   d. heard from him

**38.** I've been writing letters all day. I've already _____ fifteen.

   a. been writing

   b. written

   d. wrote

   d. have written

**39.** It's 8:30 and the musicians _____ playing yet.

   a. haven't begun

   b. hadn't been beginning

   c. hadn't begun

   d. have begun

**40.** Vicky _____ hasn't decided where she's going to go on her vacation.

   a. yet

   b. still

   c. already

   d. never

## WHICH WORD?

Tony and Sue Compton [ (had)    have    have had ] to cancel their trip to Spain

last week. It was a shame because they [ are    had    had been ]⁴¹ planning it for a

long time. Tony [ has    had    is ]⁴² been working very hard to save money, and

[ so    either    neither ]⁴³ had Sue. They [ already    had    have ]⁴⁴ also bought

new suitcases and some new clothes. Unfortunately, Sue's boss said that because it

[ hadn't    hasn't    had ]⁴⁵ become very busy at the office lately, Sue wouldn't be able

to take a vacation.

Tony and Sue are very upset because they [ haven't    won't have    weren't ]⁴⁶

been able to go on a trip for a [ several years    long time    few years ago ]⁴⁷ .

In fact, Sue is so upset that she's considering [ to quit    quit    quitting ]⁴⁸ her job and

looking [ for    after    through ]⁴⁹ a new one. She's sure she can find a new job

soon, but [ so does Tom    Tom isn't    Tom does, too ]⁵⁰ .

## CHAPTER 1

### CHOOSE

1. c
2. d
3. b
4. b
5. a
6. c
7. b
8. d
9. a
10. c

### CHOOSE

11. b
12. c
13. d
14. a
15. c

### WHAT'S THE RESPONSE?

16. a
17. d
18. b
19. b
20. c

### WHICH WORD?

21. does
22. all the time
23. wants
24. tells her she
25. says she's

## CHAPTER 2

### CHOOSE

1. b
2. d
3. c
4. d
5. a

### WHAT'S THE REASON?

6. d
7. a
8. b
9. c
10. b

### WHAT'S THE RESPONSE?

11. c
12. d
13. a
14. c
15. b

### CHOOSE

16. c
17. d
18. b
19. c
20. b

### WHAT'S THE WORD?

21. didn't
22. played
23. was
24. talking
25. wasn't

## CHAPTER 3

### CHOOSE

1. b
2. d
3. b
4. c
5. a
6. a
7. c
8. b
9. d
10. a

### CHOOSE

11. a
12. b
13. d
14. b
15. a

### WHOSE IS IT?

16. b
17. d
18. a
19. d
20. c

### WHICH WORD?

21. now
22. will
23. for
24. hour
25. later

## CHAPTER 4

### CHOOSE

1. b
2. d
3. c
4. b
5. a
6. c
7. d
8. b
9. a
10. d

### CHOOSE

11. c
12. b
13. d
14. d
15. b

### CHOOSE

16. a
17. b
18. a
19. d
20. c

### WHAT'S THE WORD?

21. haven't
22. wasn't
23. hasn't
24. have
25. already

## CHAPTER 5

### CHOOSE

1. a
2. b
3. b
4. a
5. b

### CHOOSE

6. a
7. c
8. d
9. b
10. d

### CHOOSE

11. d
12. b
13. c
14. b
15. a

### CHOOSE

16. b
17. c
18. b
19. a
20. d

### WHAT'S THE WORD?

21. for
22. since
23. didn't
24. haven't
25. don't

# MID-BOOK TEST

### Choose

| | |
|---|---|
| 1. c | 11. b |
| 2. a | 12. c |
| 3. b | 13. b |
| 4. d | 14. d |
| 5. a | 15. a |
| 6. c | 16. c |
| 7. d | 17. a |
| 8. b | 18. b |
| 9. c | 19. c |
| 10. a | 20. b |

### Choose

| | |
|---|---|
| 21. c | 31. d |
| 22. c | 32. c |
| 23. a | 33. b |
| 24. d | 34. a |
| 25. a | 35. b |
| 26. b | 36. d |
| 27. d | 37. c |
| 28. d | 38. a |
| 29. c | 39. b |
| 30. b | 40. c |

### Which Word?

41. himself
42. was hiking
43. Since
44. has been
45. already
46. feels
47. looking
48. will
49. have called
50. in

## CHAPTER 6

### Choose

| | |
|---|---|
| 1. c | 4. b |
| 2. d | 5. d |
| 3. b | |

### Choose

| | |
|---|---|
| 6. a | 9. d |
| 7. b | 10. b |
| 8. c | |

### Choose

| | |
|---|---|
| 11. b | 16. d |
| 12. b | 17. a |
| 13. a | 18. d |
| 14. b | 19. a |
| 15. c | 20. b |

### Which Word?

21. never ridden
22. tomorrow
23. been riding
24. Have
25. been

## CHAPTER 7

### Choose

| | |
|---|---|
| 1. d | 4. d |
| 2. b | 5. b |
| 3. c | |

### Choose

| | |
|---|---|
| 6. d | 9. c |
| 7. c | 10. b |
| 8. b | |

### Choose

| | |
|---|---|
| 11. b | 14. b |
| 12. a | 15. c |
| 13. d | |

### Choose

| | |
|---|---|
| 16. a | 19. d |
| 17. b | 20. c |
| 18. b | |

### What's the Word?

21. to quit
22. working
23. to go
24. starting
25. doing

## CHAPTER 8

### Choose

| | |
|---|---|
| 1. a | 4. b |
| 2. c | 5. a |
| 3. d | |

### Choose

| | |
|---|---|
| 6. c | 9. d |
| 7. b | 10. a |
| 8. a | |

### Choose

| | |
|---|---|
| 11. c | 14. c |
| 12. a | 15. b |
| 13. d | |

### Which Word Doesn't Belong?

| | |
|---|---|
| 16. d | 19. c |
| 17. b | 20. a |
| 18. a | |

### Which Word?

21. happened
22. broke
23. to take
24. had been
25. been thinking

## CHAPTER 9

### Choose

| | |
|---|---|
| 1. c | 4. b |
| 2. b | 5. c |
| 3. d | |

### Choose

| | |
|---|---|
| 6. a | 9. d |
| 7. b | 10. a |
| 8. c | |

### Choose

| | |
|---|---|
| 11. b | 14. d |
| 12. a | 15. a |
| 13. b | |

### Choose

| | |
|---|---|
| 16. d | 19. c |
| 17. c | 20. d |
| 18. a | |

### What's the Word?

21. come over
22. hung up
23. run out of
24. take down
25. put

## CHAPTER 10

### Choose

| | |
|---|---|
| 1. a | 4. d |
| 2. c | 5. b |
| 3. a | |

## CHOOSE

| | |
|---|---|
| 6. c | 9. c |
| 7. b | 10. d |
| 8. d | |

## CHOOSE

| | |
|---|---|
| 11. c | 14. a |
| 12. b | 15. c |
| 13. d | |

## CHOOSE

| | |
|---|---|
| 16. c | 19. b |
| 17. b | 20. a |
| 18. d | |

## WHICH WORD?

21. isn't
22. doesn't
23. similar
24. and neither
25. does, too

# FINAL TEST

## CHOOSE

| | |
|---|---|
| 1. b | 21. c |
| 2. a | 22. a |
| 3. c | 23. b |
| 4. d | 24. c |
| 5. a | 25. a |
| 6. c | 26. b |
| 7. b | 27. d |
| 8. d | 28. c |
| 9. b | 29. b |
| 10. a | 30. a |
| 11. c | 31. d |
| 12. b | 32. b |
| 13. a | 33. c |
| 14. d | 34. a |
| 15. a | 35. b |
| 16. b | 36. c |
| 17. c | 37. d |
| 18. d | 38. b |
| 19. c | 39. a |
| 20. b | 40. b |

## WHICH WORD?

41. had been
42. had
43. so
44. had
45. had
46. haven't
47. long time
48. quitting
49. for
50. Tom isn't

# SIDE BY SIDE
## Chapter Test Answer Sheet

BOOK _____

CHAPTER _____

Student's Name _____ I.D. Number _____

Course _____ Teacher _____ Date _____

1  (A) (B) (C) (D)          11  (A) (B) (C) (D)

2  (A) (B) (C) (D)          12  (A) (B) (C) (D)

3  (A) (B) (C) (D)          13  (A) (B) (C) (D)

4  (A) (B) (C) (D)          14  (A) (B) (C) (D)

5  (A) (B) (C) (D)          15  (A) (B) (C) (D)

6  (A) (B) (C) (D)          16  (A) (B) (C) (D)

7  (A) (B) (C) (D)          17  (A) (B) (C) (D)

8  (A) (B) (C) (D)          18  (A) (B) (C) (D)

9  (A) (B) (C) (D)          19  (A) (B) (C) (D)

10 (A) (B) (C) (D)          20  (A) (B) (C) (D)

21 _____

22 _____

23 _____

24 _____

25 _____

# SIDE BY SIDE
## Mid-Book & Final Test Answer Sheet

**BOOK** _____

Check One:
- ☐ **MID-BOOK TEST**
- ☐ **FINAL TEST**

Student's Name _____ I.D. Number _____

Course _____ Teacher _____ Date _____

1 Ⓐ Ⓑ Ⓒ Ⓓ    11 Ⓐ Ⓑ Ⓒ Ⓓ    21 Ⓐ Ⓑ Ⓒ Ⓓ    31 Ⓐ Ⓑ Ⓒ Ⓓ

2 Ⓐ Ⓑ Ⓒ Ⓓ    12 Ⓐ Ⓑ Ⓒ Ⓓ    22 Ⓐ Ⓑ Ⓒ Ⓓ    32 Ⓐ Ⓑ Ⓒ Ⓓ

3 Ⓐ Ⓑ Ⓒ Ⓓ    13 Ⓐ Ⓑ Ⓒ Ⓓ    23 Ⓐ Ⓑ Ⓒ Ⓓ    33 Ⓐ Ⓑ Ⓒ Ⓓ

4 Ⓐ Ⓑ Ⓒ Ⓓ    14 Ⓐ Ⓑ Ⓒ Ⓓ    24 Ⓐ Ⓑ Ⓒ Ⓓ    34 Ⓐ Ⓑ Ⓒ Ⓓ

5 Ⓐ Ⓑ Ⓒ Ⓓ    15 Ⓐ Ⓑ Ⓒ Ⓓ    25 Ⓐ Ⓑ Ⓒ Ⓓ    35 Ⓐ Ⓑ Ⓒ Ⓓ

6 Ⓐ Ⓑ Ⓒ Ⓓ    16 Ⓐ Ⓑ Ⓒ Ⓓ    26 Ⓐ Ⓑ Ⓒ Ⓓ    36 Ⓐ Ⓑ Ⓒ Ⓓ

7 Ⓐ Ⓑ Ⓒ Ⓓ    17 Ⓐ Ⓑ Ⓒ Ⓓ    27 Ⓐ Ⓑ Ⓒ Ⓓ    37 Ⓐ Ⓑ Ⓒ Ⓓ

8 Ⓐ Ⓑ Ⓒ Ⓓ    18 Ⓐ Ⓑ Ⓒ Ⓓ    28 Ⓐ Ⓑ Ⓒ Ⓓ    38 Ⓐ Ⓑ Ⓒ Ⓓ

9 Ⓐ Ⓑ Ⓒ Ⓓ    19 Ⓐ Ⓑ Ⓒ Ⓓ    29 Ⓐ Ⓑ Ⓒ Ⓓ    39 Ⓐ Ⓑ Ⓒ Ⓓ

10 Ⓐ Ⓑ Ⓒ Ⓓ    20 Ⓐ Ⓑ Ⓒ Ⓓ    30 Ⓐ Ⓑ Ⓒ Ⓓ    40 Ⓐ Ⓑ Ⓒ Ⓓ

41 _____

42 _____

43 _____

44 _____

45 _____

46 _____

47 _____

48 _____

49 _____

50 _____